DEDICATION

This book is dedicated to the Patriotic Americans throughout our history who believed that liberty is the ultimate and only truly worthy purpose for mankind. For all of those who have labored and fought in wars and made the ultimate sacrifice to defend and protect this liberty, I salute you.

I also want to express my gratitude to my High School American Government teacher, Larry Little who inspired me to an even greater passion for History and Politics.

Finally, a major thanks to my wife Wanda who is a constant source of support and encouragement in my efforts to express myself and my passions.

Table of Contents

The Myth of the Moderate Democrat

How the Party of Jacksonian Democracy transitioned to Marxist Statist Collectivism

By

Larry Robinson

October 2020

PREFACE

Warning to the reader. This is not another tired regurgitation of talking points by a professional pundit. What you are about to read are FACTS and history with some pithy commentary inserted to keep you awake.

One of the big debates among the political pundits is the so-called clash between "progressive" and "moderate" wings of the Democratic Party. Within this debate the punditry dutifully labor to explain that there are significant differences between these two wings. A propaganda operation regurgitated ad nauseam by the Mainstream Media.

Well friends, are we to accept this information as fact based? This same media tells us that Conservatism has moved so far to the extreme right by comparison, which they state helps to explain why we Conservatives take issue with the concept that there are any moderate/centrist Democrats in political office today.

It's important to frame this examination with a not so subtle propaganda pronouncement from Squealer the Pig.

"Do not imagine, comrades, that leadership is a

pleasure. On the contrary, it is a deep and heavy responsibility. No one believes more firmly than Comrade Napoleon that all animals are equal. He would be only too happy to let you make your decisions for yourselves. But sometimes you might make the wrong decisions, comrades, and then where should we be? " Squealer the Pig in Animal Farm

The political talking heads are obsessed with their self-importance on "educating" us to know what "we need to know" and leave the real thinking to them.

To begin with, you will read throughout much of this book about the developing Democrat ideologies of Marxist Fascism and Communism which have battled for over the past 100 years for control of the Democratic Party. You will read as I describe how FDR, LBJ, and much of the modern Democratic Party have governed with a Marxist Fascists ideology. I will back it up with documentation. And you will also learn how a separate wing has developed which seeks to fully transition to their vision of a communist utopia.

But first you need to have a sound understanding of the term Fascism. Post WWII, Historians became revisionists and redefined Fascism as an ultra right wing ideology. Before we entered WWII, most leftists in this country and Europe enthusiastically backed both Hitler and Mussolini.

From Jonah Goldberg's Liberal Fascism: The Secret

History of the American Left, From Mussolini to the Politics of Meaning 2008

> "To understand fascism in its full expression requires putting aside Stalin's misrepresentation of the term and also look beyond the Holocaust, and instead return to the period Goldberg terms the "fascist moment," roughly 1910-35. A statist ideology, fascism uses politics as the tool to transform society from atomized individuals into an organic whole. It does so by exalting the state over the individual, expert knowledge over democracy, enforced consensus over debate, and socialism over capitalism. It is totalitarian in Mussolini's original meaning of the term, of "Everything in the State, nothing outside the State, nothing against the State." Fascism's message boils down to "Enough talk, more action!" Its lasting appeal is getting things done.
>
> In contrast, conservatism calls for limited government, individualism, democratic debate, and capitalism. Its appeal is liberty and leaving citizens alone."

Goldberg's triumph is establishing the kinship between communism, fascism, and liberalism. All derive from the same tradition that goes back to the Jacobins of the French Revolution. His revised political spectrum would focus on the role of the state and go from libertarianism to conservatism to fascism in its many guises – American, Italian, German, Russian, Chinese, Cuban, and so on.

As this listing suggests, fascism is flexible; different iterations which differ in specifics but they share "emotional or instinctual impulses." Mussolini tweaked the socialist agenda to emphasize the state; Lenin made workers the vanguard party; Hitler added race. If the German version was militaristic, the American one (which Goldberg calls *liberal fascism*) is nearly pacifist. Goldberg quotes historian Richard Pipes on this point: "Bolshevism and Fascism were heresies of socialism." He proves this confluence in two ways.

First, he offers a "secret history of the American left":

- Woodrow Wilson's Progressivism featured a "militaristic, fanatically nationalist, imperialist, racist" program, enabled by the exigencies of World War I.
- Franklin D. Roosevelt's "fascist New Deal" built on and extended Wilson's government.
- Lyndon B. Johnson's Great Society established the modern welfare state, "the ultimate fruition" (so far) of this statist tradition.
- The youthful New Left revolutionaries

of the 1960s brought about "an Americanized updating" of the European Old Right.

- Hillary Clinton hopes "to insert the state deep into family life," an essential step of the totalitarian project."

Sounds nothing like the ultra, right-wing political identity that the media, historians, and Democrats have spewed for decades to describe any Conservative or even Establishment Republicans.

One of the organizations championed by the Democrats over the past century in their quest to transform America is the American Civil Liberties Union (ACLU). Its name conjures up a suggestion of America and Apple Pie. Its charter and goals though are polar opposite of those ideals.

ACLU founded upon communist ideology

- "I am for socialism, disarmament, and ultimately, for abolishing the state itself as an instrument of violence and compulsion. I seek social ownership of property, the abolition of the propertied class, and sole control of those who produce wealth. Communism is the goal." ~**Roger Baldwin**, *Founder of the American Civil Liberties Union (ACLU), a 501(c)3 tax-exempt Foundation. From the Harvard reunion book on the 30th reunion of his class of 1905*

So, this book is written to help you understand the modern Democratic Party, its ideology, and its transition from small government Jacksonian Democracy to a radical leftist political organization. It is crucial to understand, not only its roots, but how it became the party of the Marxist left that it has become.

It is also to alert American citizens to what I consider is the real time danger to the future of our Constitutional Republic and the Natural, God-given rights of free citizens by this Radical Democratic Party.

So, buckle up and let us dive into some real history you don't hear or read in the Mainstream media.

ABOUT THE AUTHOR

I have been a "political junkie" for more than 60 years. At age 10 I got hooked on reading not just one, but two editorial pages of our local papers. One was the Los Angeles Times, in 1960 a centrist, sometimes conservative Newspaper. The other was the Orange County Register, the largest and oldest libertarian daily newspaper in the United States.

I was also influenced by living in what was considered one of the most conservative counties in the US, Orange County, California. I'm a proud Disabled Veteran who enthusiastically enlisted in the Military as a seventeen year old and began active duty on January 1, 1968.

An important caveat to help eliminate any suggestion that this is an opposition hit piece from Republicans. I'm NOT a Republican. I left the Republican Party in 1970 because I felt deceived by Nixon and the Republicans who promoted the false idea that they were conservatives. Since then the only Republican I have voted for (and proudly) is Ronald Reagan. Reagan was true conservative who unfortunately was convinced by his party to fill his administration with Rockefeller Liberal Establishment Republicans. These Establishment

Republicans pushed Reagan as he noted in his diary to often go against his conservative instincts.

So, my political reality leans towards a cross between that of a Minarchist libertarian (small l) and the Classical Liberalism of most of our Founders. I'm a passionate advocate for the sovereignty of the individual as noted by Founders like Samuel Adams.

> The natural liberty of man is to be free from any superior power on earth, and not to be under the will or legislative authority of man, but only to have the law of nature for his rule.

> In short, it is the greatest absurdity to suppose it in the power of one, or any number of men, at the entering into society, to renounce their essential natural rights, or the means of preserving those rights; when the grand end of civil government, from the very nature of its institution, is for the support, protection, and defence of those very rights; the principal of which, as is before observed, are Life, Liberty, and Property. If men, through fear, fraud, or mistake, should in terms renounce or give up any essential natural right, the eternal law of reason and the grand end of society would absolutely vacate such renunciation. The right to freedom being the gift of God Almighty, it is not in the power of man to alienate this gift and voluntarily become a slave.

> Samuel Adams The Natural Rights of the

Colonists as Men, *The Report of the Committee of Correspondence to the Boston Town Meeting, Nov. 20, 1772*

CHAPTER 1- ROOTS OF THE DEMOCRATIC PARTY

Many Americans have at least some awareness of the early divide in our nation between the Federalists and the Anti-Federalists. The Federalists were first led by most notably, Alexander Hamilton and James Madison. These men along with John Jay wrote the well-known Federalist Papers. On the opposite end were the Anti-Federalists led by Thomas Jefferson, Samuel Adams, and George Mason.

Jefferson formed a political party first known as the Republican-Democrats, later Democratic-Republicans. Madison left the Federalists and joined with Jefferson in the Democratic- Republicans. They were known for their promotion of limited government, States Rights, and the importance of Agrianism to the future of the United States.

It was Andrew Jackson who formally re-named the party, the Democratic Party in 1844. Jackson maintained the core Jeffersonian beliefs of limited government and the importance of an agrian nation.

Jacksonian Democrats viewed themselves as the guardians of the United States Constitution, political democracy, individual liberty (citizen sovereignty), and equality of economic opportunity. Jacksonian Democrats also opposed the Central Bank as UnConstitutional and highly slanted to favor the wealthy (a correct assumption).

Jackson was a flawed man who was very racist so his movement was not perfect. That is for another book as this book focuses on strict political ideology on the nature of government.

"The Democrats represented a wide range of views but shared a fundamental commitment to the Jeffersonian concept of an agrarian society. They viewed the central government as the enemy of individual liberty. The 1824 "corrupt bargain" had strengthened their suspicion of Washington politics. [...] Jacksonians feared the concentration of economic and political power. They believed that government intervention in the economy benefited special-interest groups and created corporate monopolies that favored the rich. They sought to restore the independence of the individual—the artisan and the ordinary farmer—by ending federal support of banks and corporations and restricting the use of paper currency, which they distrusted. Their definition of the proper role of government tended to be negative, and Jackson's political power was largely expressed in negative

acts. He exercised the veto more than all previous presidents combined. Jackson and his supporters also opposed reform as a movement. Reformers eager to turn their programs into legislation called for a more active government. But Democrats tended to oppose programs like educational reform mid the establishment of a public education system. They believed, for instance, that public schools restricted individual liberty by interfering with parental responsibility and undermined freedom of religion by replacing church schools"
Mary Beth Norton et al., *A People and a Nation, Volume I: to 1877* (2007) pp. 287–288.

After the Civil War, the growing industrial age saw the transformation of the United States from an agrarian society to one of industry and major cities. One of the outgrowths of this was the formation of collectivist organizing by farmers. This led to not just organizing but an entire political movement. The agrarians created the People's or Populist Party in 1892, drafted a platform, and nominated James B. Weaver for president and James G. Field for vice president. The Omaha platform of 1892 concisely documented the grievances and demands of farmers. It was also one of the most radical platforms to this point in American history. Among other things, it called for government ownership and operation of the railroad, telephone, and telegraph systems.

In addition, many of its provisions would eventually become law. For example, the Omaha Platform called for immigration restriction (adopted in 1921 and 1924), the establishment of federal income tax (adopted in 1913 with the ratification of the Sixteenth Amendment), and the direct election of US senators (also adopted in 1913 with the ratification of the Seventeenth Amendment). The platform also advocated more direct democracy by granting the people the power to submit laws through referendum and the ability to recall elected officials before their term ended. The Omaha Platform also advocated the eight-hour working day, term limits for politicians, use of secret ballots in all elections, and printing money that was not backed by gold. With the exception of government ownership of railroads and telegraph lines, nearly all of the major goals of the Populists were eventually adopted by law or custom.

In the late 19th century, the Populist Party arose out of agrarian economic and political protest, was short lived, and passed into history. At the national level, the presidential administration of Woodrow Wilson (1913-1921) and the New Deal of Franklin D. Roosevelt (1933-1945) enacted most of the Populist demands into law (footnote Farmers, the Populist Party, and Mississippi (1870-1900) Professor Kenneth G. McCarty published in Mississippi History Now)

In the midst of this movement, Democrat Grover Cleveland Alexander won the presidency in 1885 and back again in 1893 and carried control of both chambers of Congress on a platform of free market capitalism, the last Democrat to do so.

The first Democrat elected after the Civil War in 1885, our 22nd and 24th President Grover Cleveland was the only President to leave the White House and return for a second term four years later (1885-1889 and 1893-1897)

> The Transformation of 1896 meant the end of America's great laissez-faire, hard-money libertarian party. The Democratic Party was no longer the party of Jefferson, Jackson, and Cleveland. With no further political embodiment for laissez-faire in existence, and with both parties offering "an echo not a choice," public interest in politics steadily declined. A power vacuum was left in American politics for the new corporate statist ideology of progressivism, which swept both parties (and created a short-lived Progressive Party) in America after 1900.

> The Progressive Era of 1900–1918 fastened a welfare-warfare state on America that has set the mold for the rest of the 20th century. Statism arrived after 1900 not because of inflation or deflation, but because a unique set of conditions had destroyed the Democrats as a laissez-faire

party and left a power vacuum for the triumph of the new ideology of compulsory cartelization through a partnership of big government, business, unions, technocrats, and intellectuals.

excerpted from A History of Money and Banking in the United States, part 1, "The History of Money and Banking Before the 20th Century" (2002).

The first Socialist Party of America (SP) was subsequently founded by a group of Populists disillusioned by the People's Party fusion with the Democrats (miserably defeated in the 1896 presidential election). As a candidate for the presidency, Socialist Eugene V Debs consistently received his highest tallies in rural areas. States such as Minnesota and Virginia prided themselves on energetic worker-farmer alliances in the 1920s. In 1924, the Socialist Party endorsed the Wisconsin populist Robert La Follette's presidential run.

CHAPTER 2- 20TH CENTURY WILSONIAN TRANSFORMATION OF THE DEMOCRATIC PARTY

The first president to embrace the Farmers Populist Party Marxist ideology was Woodrow Wilson. He was the architect of the "living Constitution" doctrine that sought to undermine the very principles of our Constitutional Republic

In The New Freedom, Wilson said:

"All that progressives ask or desire is permission—in an era when "development," "evolution," is the scientific word—to interpret the Constitution according to the Darwinian principle; all they ask is recognition of the fact that a nation is a living thing and not a machine."

(pages 46-48) {Note, this book is a collection of speeches}

In his book "Constitutional Government in the United States", President Woodrow Wilson has this to say:(page 16)

> To inquire into such matters is to make intimate approach to the very essence of constitutional government; but we approach that essence still more intimately when we turn from the community, from the nation, and from the assembly which represents it, to the individual. **No doubt a great deal of nonsense has been talked about the inalienable rights of the individual, and a great deal that was mere vague sentiment and pleasing speculation has been put forward as fundamental principle.**

Wilson made it clear that he considered the Founders wrong about the principles of Supreme Law and Enumerated Powers. Wilson questioned the very fundamentals - for Wilson it's not an issue of seeing the constitution amended because one or two things are wrong, the whole thing is wrong and needs to be scrapped. Natural law is wrong, Unalienable Rights are wrong. Unrestricted individual enterprise is wrong.   In Wilson's view (and all subsequent "progressive" Democrats), Madison, Jefferson, Samuel Adams, et al and their view of restraining Government is not only wrong, but that the individual and their interests and rights are subservient to the "needs" of the State Collective. Wilson became the model for the view of much of the modern Democratic Party and Liberal Justices in the Courts for this "living Constitution" aberrational ideology. Barack Obama noted that Wilson was an inspiration to him for his own living Constitution beliefs.

In the 1920s a much under-appreciated president Coolidge came along to briefly halt this leftist destruction of our Constitutional Republic

Calvin Coolidge (1923-1929) 30th President of the United States was dedicated to restoring the values of the Founders to the United States in both moral and Constitutional terms

By the time the disaster of the Great Depression hit the country, Coolidge was in retirement. Before his death in January 1933, he confided to an old friend a remark that many of us on the conservative side feel today, "... I feel I no longer fit in with these times.

CHAPTER 3- FDR OVERTURNS THE CONSTITUTION

The next leap forward in the evolution of the Democratic Party from libertarian-free market-limited government classic liberalism, was Franklin Delano Roosevelt's revolutionary change of our system of government and the end of free market capitalism. FDR is lauded by revisionist liberal historians and most Democrats as the President who "saved America".

Nothing could be further from the truth when viewed from the lens of objective analysis. FDR ran for President claiming to be a States rights candidate, and warning that Hoover's policies would lead to socialism. FDR's chameleon campaign became an example for all deceitful Democratic campaigns. Once elected, FDR proceeded to do everything he claimed to be against.

FDR implemented Marxist Fascism in the United States. He implemented the policies of the Communist Manifesto and Mussolini's Fascist Italy in creating the welfare state. He violated the Constitution repeatedly to usurp the separation of powers between Federal, State, and the people guaranteed by the 10th Amendment.

In his 1936 speech known as "Rendezvous with Destiny", Roosevelt announced a further motive for his New Deal programs: preserving democracy and capitalism. But it is a view that is entirely representative of Fascism or "Social Democracies". It had nothing to do with our founding principles.

Roosevelt was a devious politician as most are in reality. He disliked political labels, especially those of Fascism and Socialism. But his policies were the very thing he vocally opposed.

FDR himself referred to Mussolini and Stalin as "blood brothers," and spoke of having private contacts with Mussolini. "Mussolini," he said, "is interested in what we are doing, and I am struck by how much of his doubtless honest programs to reform Italy he has accomplished."

FDRs longstanding love of Fascism

Long before he entered national politics, FDR was already enamored with elements of Fascism

As early as 1912, FDR himself praised the Prussian-German model: "They passed beyond the liberty of the individual to do as he pleased with his own property and found it necessary to check this liberty for the benefit of the freedom of the whole people," he said in an address to the People's Forum of Troy, New York.

In the North American Review in 1934, the progressive writer Roger Shaw described the New Deal as "Fascist means to gain liberal ends." He wasn't hallucinating. FDR's adviser Rexford Tugwell wrote in his diary that Mussolini had done "many of the things which seem to me necessary." Lorena Hickok, a close confidante of Eleanor Roosevelt who lived in the White House for a spell, wrote approvingly of a local official who had said, "If [President] Roosevelt were actually a dictator, we might get somewhere." She added that if she were younger, she'd like to lead "the Fascist Movement in the United States."

At the National Recovery Administration (NRA), the cartel-creating agency at the heart of the early New Deal, one report declared forthrightly, "The Fascist Principles are very similar to those we have been evolving here in America."

Roosevelt himself called Mussolini "admirable" and professed that he was "deeply impressed by what he has accomplished." The admiration was mutual. In a laudatory review of Roosevelt's 1933 book Looking Forward, Mussolini wrote, "Reminiscent of Fascism is the principle that the state no longer leaves the economy to its own devices.... Without question, the mood accompanying this sea change resembles that of Fascism."

The chief Nazi newspaper, *Volkischer Beobachter*, repeatedly praised "Roosevelt's adoption of National Socialist strains of thought in his economic and social policies" and "the development toward an authoritarian state" based on the "demand that collective good be put before individual self-interest."

In 1935 former President Herbert Hoover was using phrases like "Fascist regimentation" in discussing the New Deal. A decade later, he wrote in his memoirs that "the New Deal introduced to Americans the spectacle of Fascist dictation to business, labor and agriculture," and that measures such as the Agricultural Adjustment Act, "in their consequences of control of products and markets, set up an uncanny Americanized parallel with the agricultural regime of Mussolini and Hitler." In 1944, in *The Road to Serfdom*, the economist F.A. Hayek warned that economic planning could lead to totalitarianism. He cautioned Americans and Britons not to think that there was something uniquely evil about the German soul. National Socialism, he said, drew on collectivist ideas that had permeated the Western world for a generation or more.

In 1973 one of the most distinguished American historians, John A. Garraty of Columbia University, created a stir with his article "The New Deal, National Socialism, and the Great Depression." Garraty was an admirer of Roosevelt but couldn't help noticing, for instance, the parallels between the Civilian Conservation Corps and similar programs in Germany."

https://www.cato.org/publications/commentary/hitler-mussolini-roosevelt

Secretary of the Interior Harold Ickes thought that : "what we are doing in this country is analogous to what is being done in Russia and even under Hitler in Germany. The only thing is that we do it methodically."

The Failure Of Fdr's Fascist Model In America

Unemployment dropped to 18 percent in 1935, 14 percent in 1936, and even lower in 1937. But by 1938, it was back up to nearly 20 percent as the economy slumped again. The stock market crashed nearly 50 percent between August 1937 and March 1938. The "economic stimulus" of Franklin Delano Roosevelt's New Deal had achieved a real "first": a depression within a depression!

Perhaps the most radical aspect of the New Deal was the National Industrial Recovery Act, passed in June 1933, which created a massive new bureaucracy called the National Recovery Administration. Under the NRA, most manufacturing industries were suddenly forced into government-mandated cartels. Codes that regulated prices and terms of sale briefly transformed much of the American economy into a fascist-style arrangement, while the NRA was financed by new taxes on the very industries it controlled. Some economists have estimated that the NRA boosted the cost of doing business by an average of 40 percent — not something a depressed economy needed for recovery.

The economic impact of the NRA was immediate and powerful. In the five months leading up to the act's passage, signs of recovery were evident: factory employment and payrolls had increased by

23 and 35 percent, respectively. Then came the NRA, shortening hours of work, raising wages arbitrarily and imposing other new costs on enterprise. In the six months after the law took effect, industrial production dropped 25 percent. Benjamin M. Anderson writes, "NRA was not a revival measure. It was an anti-revival measure. … Through the whole of the NRA period industrial production did not rise as high as it had been in July 1933, before NRA came in."

Roosevelt's Civil Works Administration hired actors to give free shows and librarians to catalog archives. It even paid researchers to study the history of the safety pin, hired 100 Washington workers to patrol the streets with balloons to frighten starlings away from public buildings, and put men on the public payroll to chase tumbleweeds on windy days.

The CWA, when it was started in the fall of 1933, was supposed to be a short-lived jobs program. Roosevelt assured Congress in his State of the Union message that any new such program would be abolished within a year. "The federal government," said the president, "must and shall quit this business of relief. I am not willing that the vitality of our people be further stopped by the giving of cash, of market baskets, of a few bits of weekly work cutting grass, raking leaves, or picking up papers in the public parks." Harry Hopkins was put in charge of the agency and later said, "I've got four million at work but for God's sake, don't ask me what they are doing." The CWA came to an end within a few months but was replaced with another temporary relief program that evolved into the Works Progress Administration, or WPA, by 1935. It is known today as the very government program that gave rise to the new term, "boondoggle," because it "produced" a lot more than the 77,000 bridges and 116,000 buildings to which its advocates loved to point as evidence of its efficacy.[31]

With good reason, critics often referred to the WPA as "We Piddle Around." In Kentucky, WPA workers catalogued 350 different ways to cook spinach. The agency employed 6,000 "actors" though the nation's actors' union claimed only 4,500 members. Hundreds of WPA workers were used to collect campaign contributions for Democratic Party candidates. In Tennessee, WPA workers were fired if they refused to donate 2 percent of their wages to the incumbent governor. By 1941, only 59 percent of the WPA budget went to paying workers anything at all; the rest was sucked up in administration and overhead. The editors of The New Republic asked, "Has [Roosevelt] the moral stature to admit now that the WPA was a hasty and grandiose political gesture, that it is a wretched failure and should be abolished?"[32] The last of the WPA's projects was not eliminated until July of 1943.

http://www.fee.org/articles/great-myths-of-the-great-depression/

How Fdr Used The Courts To Push His Fascist Agenda

Within a few years of implementing the New Deal, FDR came up against a roadblock, the Supreme Court.

Over the course of the Depression, Roosevelt was pushing through legislation and, beginning in May 1935, the Supreme Court began to strike down a number of the New Deal laws. "Over the next 13 months, the court struck down more pieces of legislation than at any other time in U.S. history," Woolner says.

Roosevelt's first New Deal program—in particular, its centerpiece, the National Recovery Administration, along with parts of the Agricultural Adjustment Act—had been struck down by unanimous and near-unanimous votes.

> Dr. David B. Woolner, senior fellow and resident historian of the Roosevelt Institute and author of *The Last 100 Days: FDR at War and at Peace*

This led to FDR's famous Court Packing attempt. The Judicial Procedures Reform Bill of 1937, commonly referred to as the "court-packing plan," was Roosevelt's attempt to appoint up to six additional justices to the Supreme Court for every justice older than 70 years, 6 months, who had served 10 years or more.

It fortunately was overwhelmingly rejected by both Congress and the American people. We coincidently see the Democrats floating the same irresponsible position in 2020.

Two Supreme Court Decisions Upheld Roosevelts Attack On The Constitution's Restraint Of Government.

The First was Helvering v Davis which legitimized the Social Security Tax as a "General Tax".

Helvering v. Davis (1937). *Helvering* upheld the constitutionality of Social Security on the basis that Congress has a general power to spend on whatever it deems to be in the general welfare. This opinion single handedly gave the Federal Government the power to create a Fascist Welfare State.

The Second that also usurped the Constitution was Wickard v Filburn. This opinion gave the government virtually carte blanche to use the Commerce Clause to regulate or tax anything it wished. As noted below, two cases since have only reigned in slightly this totalitarian expansion of power. Wickard has been the cornerstone of Marxist Fascist control of everything from farming to home-based business.

Wickard marked the beginning of the Supreme Court's total deference to the claims of the US Congress to Commerce Clause powers until the 1990s. The Court's own decision, however, emphasizes the role of the democratic electoral process in confining the abuse of the power of

Congress. Wickard was the ultimate assault on Chief Justice Marshall's defining opinion that confirmed that the Federal Government was one of Enumerated Powers and that it could not go beyond what was clearly enumerated (clear stated language of the law).

According to Earl M. Maltz, *Wickard* and other New Deal decisions gave Congress "the authority to regulate private economic activity in a manner near limitless in its purview."

That remained the case until United States v Lopez (1995), which was the first decision in six decades to invalidate a federal statute on the grounds that it exceeded the power of the Congress under the Commerce Clause. The opinion described *Wickard* as "perhaps the most far reaching example of Commerce Clause authority over intrastate commerce" and judged that it "greatly expanded the authority of Congress beyond what is defined in the Constitution under that Clause."

In *Lopez*, the Court held that while Congress had broad lawmaking authority under the Commerce Clause, the power was limited and did not extend so far from "commerce" as to authorize the regulation of the carrying of handguns, especially when there was no evidence that carrying them affected the economy on a massive scale. (In a later case, United States v. Morrison, the Court ruled in 2000 that Congress could not make such laws even when there was evidence of aggregate effect.)

FDR CONCLUSIONS

While Woodrow Wilson set the stage for the so-called Progressive Democratic Ideology, FDR was the true architect of its implementation. From Obama to Bernie Sanders, they all praise FDR's vision of redistribution of wealth and totalitarian government control over free enterprise/capitalism as the model to expand upon.

CHAPTER 4- JOHN F KENNEDY- LAST DEMOCRAT WHO BELIEVED IN AMERICAN VALUES

I remember when JFK was running for president. In Orange County California where I grew up, Kennedy may have been a war hero, but he was viewed as an evil Democrat and most likely an FDR leftist.

It took many years after his death when many of his writings and speeches became publicly available, that I learned he had actually been quite conservative. In fact, I believe it was his conservativism that it appears led to the left assassinating him.

JFK was very much a forerunner of Reaganism as a conservative political ideology. He brought a combination of charisma and sound American ideals to the presidency that represent a brief glimpse of what the Democratic Party could have been. Instead as we see, they transitioned quickly back into a Marxist Collectivist Party.

Let's look at some highlights of John F Kennedy's real political philosophy

In case anyone had doubts, JFK made it clear what he thought of the left

> " I'd be very happy to tell them I'm not a liberal at all…I'm not comfortable with those people." John F Kennedy *Saturday Evening Post, June 1953*

The Media and others considered JFK a Conservative

> "A Kennedy Runs for Congress; The Boston-bred scion of a former ambassador is a fighting-Irish conservative," *Look* magazine headlined an article in its June 11, 1946, issue.
> *The Chicago Tribune* reported Kennedy's election to the Senate in 1952 by describing him as a "fighting conservative."

> On Dec. 7, 1958, Eleanor Roosevelt was asked in a television interview what she would do if she had to choose between a "conservative Democrat like Kennedy and a liberal Republican [like] Rockefeller"

> A campaign staffer and congressional aide, William Sutton, described Kennedy's political stance in the 1946 campaign as "almost ultraconservative."

> "He was more conservative than anything else,"

said a Navy friend of Kennedy's, James Reed, who went on to serve as assistant Treasury secretary in the Kennedy administration.

Kennedy's speechwriter and longtime aide, Ted Sorensen, said, "Kennedy was a fiscal conservative. Most of us and the press and historians have, for one reason or another, treated Kennedy as being much more liberal than he so regarded himself at the time... in fiscal matters, he was extremely conservative, very cautious about the size of the budget."

He Believed Our Rights Come From God, Not The State.

From JFKs inaugural address January 20,1961

"And yet the same revolutionary beliefs for which our forebears fought are still at issue around the globe--the belief that the rights of man come not from the generosity of the state but from the hand of God."

He Believed In The Same Values As Our Founders And Most Patriotic, God-Fearing Americans

"Our government was founded on the essential religious idea of integrity of the individual. It was this religious sense which inspired the authors of the Declaration of Independence: The American character has been not only religious, idealistic, and patriotic, but because of these it has been essentially individual".

"Conceived in Grecian thought, strengthened by Christian morality, and stamped indelibly into American political philosophy, the right of the individual against the State is the keystone of our Constitution. Each man is free".

Our late, lamented President was deeply inspired by this deep religious sense:

"We shall win this war, and in victory we shall seek not vengeance, but the establishment of an international order in which the spirit of Christ shall rule the hearts of men and women.

Today these basic religious ideas are challenged by atheism and materialism: at home in the cynical philosophy of many of our intellectuals, abroad in the doctrine of collectivism, which sets up the twin pillars of atheism

and materialism as the official philosophical establishment of the State.
John F Kennedy
Independence Day Oration, July 4th 1946

Kennedy like today's conservatives was concerned about growing power in Washington

"The ever expanding power of the federal government, the absorption of many of the functions that states and cities once considered to be responsibilities of their own, must now be a source of concern to all those who believe as did the great patriot, Henry Grattan that: "Control over local affairs is the essence of liberty."
John F Kennedy Commencement Address, Universtity of Notre Dame, January 29, 1950

Kennedy On Taxes And Budgets

In a speech to the Associated Business Publications Conference during the 1960 campaign, he said, "We should seek a balanced budget over the course of the business cycle with surpluses during good times more than offsetting the deficits which may be incurred during slumps. I submit that this is not a radical fiscal policy. It is a conservative policy."

John Kenneth Galbraith, the 6-foot, eight-inch tall liberal Keynesian Harvard economics professor, opposed the Kennedy tax cuts, preferring increased government spending instead. As Galbraith described it, Kennedy finally lost patience: "The president told me to shut up about my opposition to tax cuts."

> *"In today's economy, fiscal prudence and responsibility call for tax reduction even if it temporarily enlarges the federal deficit – why reducing taxes is the best way open to us to increase revenues."*
> *John F. Kennedy, Jan. 21, 1963, annual message to the Congress: "The Economic Report Of The President"*

> *"It is no contradiction – the most important single thing we can do to stimulate investment in today's economy is to raise consumption by major reduction of individual income tax rates."*
> *John F. Kennedy, Jan. 21, 1963, annual message to the Congress: "The Economic Report Of The President"*

> *"Our tax system still siphons out of the private economy too large a share of personal and business purchasing power and reduces the incentive for risk, investment and effort –*

thereby aborting our recoveries and stifling our national growth rate."
John F. Kennedy, Jan. 24, 1963, message to Congress on tax reduction and reform, House Doc. 43, 88th Congress, 1st Session.

On Foreign Policy And Military Defense

JFK was staunchly anti-Communist and had an aggressive view of the necessity of American Military Strength combined with a strong American Self Interest view of Foreign Policy

On foreign policy, Kennedy believed the U.S. had to take an active role in the world. His foreign policy was hawkish from the beginning, starting with the Bay of Pigs invasion and continuing with American intervention in South Vietnam and the Cuban Missile Crisis. JFK would routinely stress the need for a military buildup.

On March 28, 1961, Kennedy gave a special message to Congress calling for an increase of $650 million for the defense budget.

> He declared that "any potential aggressor contemplating an attack on any part of the Free World with any kind of weapons, conventional or nuclear, must know that our response will be suitable, selective, swift and effective. While he may be uncertain of its exact nature and location, there must be no uncertainty about our determination and capacity to take whatever steps are necessary to meet our obligations."

At a speech in November 1961 in Los Angeles, he informed his supporters that the administration "developed five additional combat divisions" and "will have a substantially increased number of Polaris submarines by 1963 and 1964 than we would have had." In terms of the space race, Kennedy said he did not "believe that we want to permit the Soviet Union to dominate space, with all that it might mean to our peace and security in coming years."

Under Kennedy, defense spending would increase from $64.54 billion in 1961 to $69.99 billion in 1963. The number of active-duty military personnel would increase by about 200,000 from 1961 to 1963. He bolstered old allies and aligned the U.S. with new ones like Israel, ending an arms embargo and selling them surface-to-air missiles for protection.

Again from Kennedy's 1961 Inaugural Address

Finally, to those nations who would make themselves our adversary, we offer not a pledge but a request: that both sides begin anew the quest for peace, before the dark powers of destruction unleashed by science engulf all humanity in planned or accidental self-destruction.

We dare not tempt them with weakness. For only when our arms are sufficient beyond doubt can we be certain beyond doubt that they will never be employed.

But neither can two great and powerful groups of nations take comfort from our present course—both sides overburdened by the cost of modern weapons, both rightly alarmed by the steady spread of the deadly atom, yet both racing to alter that uncertain balance of terror that stays the hand of mankind's final war.

Let every nation know, whether it wishes us well or ill, that we shall pay any price, bear any burden, meet any hardship, support any friend, oppose any foe, in order to assure the survival and the success of liberty.

This much we pledge—and more.

Finally to those nations who would make themselves our adversary, we offer not a pledge, but a request: that both sides begin anew the quest for peace, before the dark powers of destruction, unleashed by science engulf all humanity in planned or accidental self-destruction.

We dare not tempt them with weakness. For only when our arms are sufficient beyond doubt can we be certain beyond doubt that they will never be employed

So let us begin anew—remembering on both sides that civility is not a sign of weakness, and sincerity is always subject to proof. Let us never negotiate out of fear. But let us never fear to negotiate.

HIS VIEWS ON COMMUNISM

Asked by one journalist why he was pressing for a perjury charge against a labor leader, he said the man had led "a commie strike."

Richard Nixon recalled in his memoir that during the 1960 presidential debates, "Kennedy conveyed the image — to 60 million people — that he was tougher on Castro and communism than I was."

At the Mormon Tabernacle in 1960, Kennedy said, "The enemy is the communist system itself — implacable, insatiable, unceasing in its drive for world domination."

At Berlin in 1963, Kennedy said, "There are some who say in Europe and elsewhere we can work with the Communists. Let them come to Berlin."

JFK considered himself a friend and ally of Joseph McCarthy, the patriot against Communism in the United States (the same McCarthy that Democrats loathe so much, his name is like a curse word when they use it).

JFK liked the fact that McCarthy went after the "elites" in the State Department whom JFK regarded with contempt. Even before McCarthy made accusations against the State Department of subversion, JFK had already aligned himself with the militant anti-communists who blamed the Truman State Department for the "loss" of China.

JFK DECLARED ON THE HOUSE
FLOOR IN JANUARY 1949.

"The responsibility for the failure of our foreign policy in the Far East rests squarely with the White House and the Department of State." [14]

Small wonder then, that at the same Harvard seminar where he cheered Nixon's victory to the Senate, that JFK expressed the view that McCarthy "may have something" to his charges of domestic subversion that had by then become vocal

Deep personal bonds developed between JFK and McCarthy by the time McCarthy reached the peak of his power in 1952 and 1953. Not only had McCarthy been a frequent guest at the Kennedy compound in Hyannis, but McCarthy had also dated two Kennedy sisters, first Eunice (the mother of Maria Shriver) and then Pat (who later married actor Peter Lawford). McCarthy was invited to the wedding reception for Eunice and Sargent Shriver, and even presented Eunice with a silver cigarette case inscribed "To Eunice and Bob from one who lost." Thomas Reeves, *The Life and Times of Joe McCarthy* (New York, 1982), 203

McCarthy's ties with Bobby Kennedy were forged when he gave RFK a job as minority counsel to his Senate committee investigating domestic communism. Though RFK would later have an intense falling out with McCarthy's other counsel Roy Cohn, the younger Kennedy brother would maintain a deep loyalty to a man he loved enough to make the godfather of his first child. In 1955

JFK WAS STRONGLY PRO-LIFE AND ANTI-ABORTION

As a senator, Kennedy was asked, "Do you see any hope at all of slowing up the rate of population increase?" Kennedy's reply was somewhat dismissive. "Now, on the question of limiting population: As you know the Japanese have been doing it very vigorously, through abortion, which I think would be repugnant to all Americans."

Byron White (left), a Kennedy Supreme Court appointee, was one of only two justices who dissented against the 1973 decision in *Roe v. Wade* that found women had the constitutional right to an abortion. White's dissent accused the Roe majority of "interposing a constitutional barrier to state efforts to protect human life."

JFK WAS NOT A PUPPET OF UNIONS
AS ARE TODAY'S DEMOCRATS

As a senator, one of Kennedy's main efforts was a campaign against what he called "the cancer of labor racketeering." He criticized union leaders who he said "practice extortion, shakedowns, and bribery."

JFK IN CONCLUSION

Despite the attempts of the Media, Historians, and the Democratic Party to portray John F Kennedy as a champion of liberalism, an objective review of his history shows Kennedy to be a center-right politician. His views would be labeled as extreme right-wing by today's Democrats. His strong beliefs in patriotism, individualism, and religious faith as essential to American character would find no acceptance among Democrats. His strong stands against Communism, centralized power in Washington, and his anti-abortion views are polar opposite of today's Democratic Party.

They believed he had to be eliminated as a threat to their power and their ideology. Assassination allowed them to falsely make him a liberal martyr.

CHAPTER 5- LBJ EXPANDS FDR FASCISM WITH THE GREAT SOCIETY

"Your imagination and your initiative and your indignation will determine whether we build a society where progress is the servant of our needs, or a society where old values and new visions are buried under unbridled growth. For in your time, we have the opportunity to move not only toward the rich society and the powerful society, but upward to the Great Society."

President Lyndon Baines Johnson, Commencement Address, University of Michigan,
May 22, 1964

In announcing the "Great Society," Johnson set out a half-century time-frame to judge its success. "The challenge of the next half century," he declared, "is whether we will have the wisdom to use [America's] wealth to enrich and elevate our national life, and to advance the quality of our American civilization....

For in your time we have the opportunity to move not only toward the rich society and the powerful society, but upward to the Great Society."

Johnson had a vision to dramatically expand the Marxist, Redistribution of Wealth ideology of FDR.

Today, America has over 70 welfare programs to aid the poor and has spent more than $22 trillion on the so-called War On Poverty. One would think such massive resources and efforts would have eradicated --- or greatly lessened --- poverty in America.

The poverty rate was 14 percent in 1965. In 2018, 13.1% of the U.S. population had income below the poverty level, down from 13.4% in 2017.

Source: https://www.census.gov/library/stories/2019/09/percentage-of-people-in-poverty-dropped-fifth-consecutive-year.html

The Congressional Research Services notes that in 1962, before the Great Society began, mandatory spending was only 30% of the federal budget. Today that figure is nearly 60% and climbing. Social Security takes up the largest portion of the mandatory spending dollars. In fact, Social Security demands $1.046 trillion of the total $2.739-trillion mandatory spending budget. It also includes programs like unemployment benefits and welfare. Medicare is currently underfunded, relying on general tax dollars to make up the difference. Only a portion of the $625-billion Medicare budget is covered by Medicare taxes.

One of the other unintended consequences of the Great Society Welfare State is the exponential expansion of single parent (mostly women, mostly black women) households

In its annual "America's Families and Living Arrangements" data collection, the Bureau examined marriage and family, the living arrangements of older adults and other household characteristics.

It found that a majority of the 73.7 million American children under age 18 live in families with two parents (69 percent)—a decrease from 88 percent in 1960. Of those 50.7 million children living in families with two parents, 47.7 million live with two married parents and 3 million live with two unmarried parents.

Broken down by race, however, the statistics show stark differences. The percentage of White children under 18 who live with both parents almost doubles that of Black children, according to the data. While 74.3 percent of all White children below the age of 18 live with both parents, only 38.7 percent of African-American minors can say the same.
https://afro.com/census-burear-higher-percentage-black-children-live-single-mothers/

I won't even discuss the failed leadership by LBJ in Vietnam. Suffice it to say, LBJ tied the hands of the military to prevent any opportunity to defeat communism in South East Asia.

In an address delivered in 1983, President Ronald Reagan denounced the Great Society as a bundle of expensive and failed initiatives that contributed to, rather than alleviated, suffering. Johnson's legacy reinforced what Reagan called the "central political error of our time": the flawed notion that "government and bureaucracy" were the "primary vehicle for social change."

CHAPTER 6- JIMMY CARTER AND BILL CLINTON'S MIXED MESSAGES

Jimmy Carter ran in 1976 as a "New Way" Democrat who supposedly was centrist and not bound to the leftist ideology of most of the Democratic Party. The reality was much different.

In foreign policy, his appeasement and love of Islamic Jihadists and Communist Governments led to the fall of Iran, expanded the Arab wars against Israel, and propped up Communist Governments in the Western Hemisphere (ie. Nicaragua and Cuba)

On Domestic Issues, he and his leftist Congress created the Departments of Education and Energy. His failure to take strong stands led to stagnated economic growth, rampant inflation and high interest rates.

Carter expanded upon Nixon's visit to China in 1972 by normalizing relations with Red China without any diplomatic concessions in return. He is the singular president responsible for China's expansion both regionally and globally. Consequently, Carter moved to acknowledge the Chinese government and Taiwan as a part of China, 'There is but one China, and Taiwan is a part of China' (Carter, 1978). In doing this, Carter crushed Taiwan's hope for international support for its sovereignty and independence. His administration left Taiwan to the mercy of China where the US had intelligence that human rights abuses were rife. Carter choose appeasement of Communism rather than taking a firm stance towards a positive relationship with China through strength.

In a 1978 speech, Carter noted China's rising power and high population was only "reality" and that it was in "normalization .... will contribute to our own national interest" (Carter, 1978). This false choice is echoed today by Joe Biden.

Nowhere is Carter's foreign policy failure more notable than with Iran (later echoed by Obama). Iran had been a staunch ally under the rule of the Shah. The Shah was anxious to maintain this relationship and during Carter's presidency introduced many reforms to loosen his authoritarian rule.

Carter's appeasement of leftist pressure by members of Congress led him to abandon the Shah, falsely assuming the Ayatollahs would not be as extremist as some warned.

This led to the capture and hostage of Americans for more than a year

Just to refresh your memory (or as a first time education): The Iranian hostage crisis (1978-1979) in which Islamic militants in Iran seized 66 American citizens at the US Embassy in Tehran and held 52 of them hostage for more than a year.   The crisis, which took place during the chaotic aftermath of Iran's Islamic Revolution and its overthrow of the Pahlavi monarchy, has had dramatic effects on US domestic politics and US-Iranian relations ever since. Several of the hostage takers would later become Iranian political and military leaders including Mahmoud Ahmadinejad (who would become President of Iran). Hossein Sheikholeslam, the former Iranian ambassador to Syria, and Iranian vice president for women and global affairs Massoumeh Ebtekar.

Carter's approach to "progressive" governance produced a weakened United States in military strength and foreign policy.

Domestically, Carter was thoroughly a progressive. He used the mid 1970s energy crisis to create a powerful new department of Energy to further leftist goals.

On April 21, 1977, President Jimmy Carter

delivered his Address to the Nation on National Energy Policy, better known as the "Moral Equivalent of War" speech. Seated behind his ornate desk in the Oval Office and wearing a sober pinstriped suit, he offered a litany of dark predictions:

1. "The oil and natural gas we rely on for 75 percent of our energy are running out."
2. "Unless profound changes are made to lower oil consumption, we now believe that early in the 1980s the world will be demanding more oil than it can produce."
3. "World oil production can probably keep going up for another six or eight years. But some time in the 1980s, it can't go up much more. Demand will overtake production. We have no choice about that."
4. "We can't substantially increase our domestic production…"
5. "Within ten years we would not be able to import enough oil—from any country, at any acceptable price."
6. "If we fail to act soon, we will face an economic, social and political crisis that will threaten our free institutions."
7. ALL of his predictions were wrong.

Carter based them upon the predictions of Environmental Activists who opposed domestic production of Gas, Oil, and Coal.

https://fee.org/articles/jimmy-carter-and-the-energy-crisis-that-never-happened/

On August 4, 1977, President Jimmy Carter signed the U.S. Department of Energy (DOE) Organization Act (Public Law 95-91), centralizing the responsibilities of the Federal Energy Administration, the Energy Research and Development Administration, the Federal Power Commission and other energy-related government programs into a single presidential all powerful cabinet-level department.

His other radical move was purely to obtain the support of the NEA (the National Education Association), the largest Teachers Union.

It was universally understood that education was Constitutionally enumerated as a power for State and local governments to determine

President Andrew Johnson signed the Department of Education Act in 1867 reluctantly, after he had been assured it was harmless. It was a meek agency. Congress authorized it to have just four employees – besides Commissioner Barnard, there were three clerks – and limited its powers to "collecting such statistics and facts as shall show the condition and progress of education in the United States." The DOE also was to publish useful information on the "organization and operation" of school systems and "promote the case of education throughout the country."

Even with these limits, many in Congress hated the Department. They saw its existence as an unconstitutional power grab and worried that its data-gathering authority gave Washington a new and dangerous kind of leverage. Rep. Andrew Rogers (D-N.J.) declared: "I am content, sir, to leave this matter of education where our fathers left it, where the history of our country left it, to the schools systems of the different towns, cities and states...[This legislation] proposes to collect such statistics which will give a controlling power over the schools systems of the states."

https://www.politico.com/agenda/story/2015/09/department-of-education-history-000235/

Creating the Department of Education was Carter's fulfillment of a 1976 presidential campaign promise, when he earned the endorsement of the largest labor union in the United States—the National Education Association (NEA).

The NEA gave its first presidential endorsement ever in 1976, when Walter Mondale promised them, at an NEA annual meeting, that the Carter administration would form an education department. At the 1976 Democratic National Convention, more delegates — 180 — belonged to the NEA than any other group of any kind. They endorsed Carter again for 1980. They have endorsed every Democratic Nominee ever since.

Domestically, we had high inflation and interest rates and economic malaise. It took Ronald Reagan to at least to current date, break the back of inflation and high interest rates.

Bill Clinton and 3<u>rd</u> Way Politics

The 1992 Presidential Campaign race featured the usual leftist Democrats and a young Governor from Arkansas, Bill Clinton. Clinton ran on a so-called Third Way ideology which attempted to merge elements of socialism with capitalism and an appeal to centrist voters.

Third Way politics is an ideological development from Anthony Giddens. In works such as *Consequences of Modernity* (1990), *Modernity and Self-Identity* (1991), *The Transformation of Intimacy* (1992), *Beyond Left and Right* (1994) and *The Third Way: The Renewal of Social Democracy* (1998). In *Beyond Left and Right*, Giddens criticizes market socialism and constructs a six-point framework for a reconstituted radical politics includes the following values:

1. Repair damaged solidarities.

2. Recognize the centrality of life politics.

3. Accept that active trust implies generative politics.

4. Embrace dialogic democracy.

5. Rethink the welfare state.

6. Confront violence.

In *The Third Way*, Giddens provides the framework within which the Third Way, also termed by Giddens as the radical centre, is justified. In addition, it supplies a broad range of policy proposals aimed at what Giddens calls the "progressive centre-left" in British politics.

From the summary of Beyond Left and Right:

How should one understand the nature and possibilities of political radicalism today? The political radical is normally thought of as someone who stands on the left, opposing backward-looking conservatism. In the present day, however, the left has turned defensive, while the right has become radical, advocating the free play of market forces no matter what obstacles of tradition or custom stand in their way.

What explains such a curious twist of perspective? In answering this question, Giddens develops a new framework for radical politics, drawing on what he calls "philosophic conservatism," but applying this outlook in the service of values normally associated with the left. The ecological crisis is at the core of this analysis, but is understood by Giddens in an unconventional way—as a response to a world in which modernity has run up against its independently human intervention, and the end of tradition, combined with the impact of globalization, are the forces which now have to be confronted, made use of and coped with.

Beyond Left and Right by Anthony Giddons-Stanford University Press; 1st Edition (January 1, 1994

Clinton's campaign was successful primarily because of two factors. One was his charismatic personality. Clinton was a charmer who had a lot of appeal to female voters. But of greater consequence was the 3rd party candidacy of Ross Perot. Conservatives had always been suspicious of George W Bush. Most considered him to be more of a Rockefeller Republican. Perot ran on returning fiscal responsibility and as a man of common business sense. Perot got nearly 20% of the vote which seriously damaged Bush and Clinton ended up winning with only 42% of the popular vote.

Clinton had a staff that was reflective of the leftists in the Democratic Party and they with Al Gore as Vice President pushed Clinton towards the usual Democratic policies of higher taxes, regulations and nominating liberals like Ruth Bader Ginsburg on the Supreme Court.

The 1994 Republican takeover of the House of Representatives after 50 plus years of Democratic control pushed Clinton to embrace the appearance of more centrist 3rd Way policies.

Clinton in his 1996 State of the Union angered the left with these words

> We must answer here three fundamental questions: First, how do we make the American Dream of opportunity for all a reality for all Americans who are willing to work for it? Second, how do we preserve our old and enduring values as we move into the future? And, third, how do we meet these challenges together, as one America?

> We know big government does not have all the answers. We know there's not a program for every problem. We have worked to give the American people a smaller, less bureaucratic government in Washington. And we have to give the American people one that lives within its means.

> The era of big government is over. But we cannot go back to the time when our citizens were left to fend for themselves. Instead, we must go forward as one America, one nation working together to meet the challenges we face together. Self-reliance and teamwork are not opposing

virtues; we must have both.

I believe our new, smaller government must work in an old-fashioned American way, together with all of our citizens through state and local governments, in the workplace, in religious, charitable and civic associations. Our goal must be to enable all our people to make the most of their own lives -- with stronger families, more educational opportunity, economic security, safer streets, a cleaner environment in a safer world.

To improve the state of our Union, we must ask more of ourselves, we must expect more of each other, and we must face our challenges together.

Here, in this place, our responsibility begins with balancing the budget in a way that is fair to all Americans. There is now broad bipartisan agreement that permanent deficit spending must come to an end.

https://clintonwhitehouse2.archives.gov/WH/New/other/sotu.html

CARTER/CLINTON GIVE AWAY
THE PANAMA CANAL

President Clinton admitted to reporters in a 1999 press conference that the Communist Chinese will, in fact, run the Panama Canal when the United States pulls all of its troops out and relinquishes control of the vital waterway Jan. 1, 2000.

Clinton addressed the issue of the imminent U.S. surrender of the American-built multi-billion-dollar canal.

> "I supported it at the time and I still support it," Clinton said, referring to the controversial 1978 treaties signed by then-President Jimmy Carter and Panamanian dictator Omar Torrijos, requiring U.S. surrender of the Panama Canal to the Central American nation at the century's end.

> "I think it's the right thing to do," the president said.

> Clinton noted that the United States would be represented in Panama for the year-end change-over by former President Carter, whose administration negotiated the

treaties, and Secretary of State Madeleine Albright. Carter "deserves enormous credit" for winning Senate passage of the treaties, which, Clinton added, were "very controversial, immensely unpopular. A lot of the members of the Senate ... had their seats put in peril over it," the Associated Press reported.

As the time approached, congressional and military warnings about America's imminent loss of control of the canal were dismissed and scoffed at by the Clinton administration.

During yesterday's announcement, Clinton, once again, at first brushed off concerns -- voiced most recently by former Joint Chiefs of Staff Chairman Adm. Thomas Moorer -- that China is preparing to take over the canal once the United States leaves. Moorer has asserted publicly that China plans to seize control of the canal through a Hong Kong company, Hutchison Whampoa Ltd. -- a firm widely believed to have close links to the Chinese military -- which has won rights to operate ports on both ends of the canal.

After much pressure and prodding President Clintonopenly admitted that China will, indeed, control the Panama Canal after Dec. 31.

"I think the Chinese will in fact be bending over backwards to make sure that they run

it in a competent and able and fair manner,"
Clinton said.

http://www.worldnetdaily.com/news/article.asp?
ARTICLE_ID=17269

Clinton was a smart politician who recognized the direction of the political winds and even with his impeachment, worked to implement many of the policy recommendations of the Conservative, Newt Gingrich led "Contract With America". Spending increases were reduced, Capital Gains Tax Cuts were passed, and Clinton took a strong stance on combatting Illegal Immigration.
These political moves gave Clinton broad approval among Americans even with the knowledge of his sexual scandals revealed by the Impeachment. And the Senate recognized this fact by refusing to remove him from office.

We will likely never see any Democrat successfully run for national office on the type of platform and policies that enabled Clinton to have what many deem a successful presidency.

CHAPTER 7-
BARACK OBAMA'S FUNDAMENTAL TRANSFORMATION OF AMERICA

"Barack Obama October 28, 2008 campaign visit to Columbia, Missouri:

"Now, Mizzou, I just have two words for you tonight: five days. Five days. After decades of broken politics in Washington, and eight years of failed policies from George W. Bush, and 21 months of a campaign that's taken us from the rocky coast of Maine to the sunshine of California, we are five days away from fundamentally transforming the United States of America.

"In five days, you can turn the page on policies that put greed and irresponsibility on Wall Street before the hard work and sacrifice of folks on Main Street. In five days, you can choose policies that invest in our middle class, and create new jobs, and grow this economy, so that everyone has a chance to succeed, not just the CEO, but the secretary and janitor, not just the factory owner, but the men and women on the factory floor."

Barack Obama always viewed himself to be a "pragmatic" Marxist who takes things incrementally. But Marxist Revolution was always his ideological foundation. Looking back on his 8 years as president and his time in State Government and as a Senator, it's easy now to see how this drove his actions.

Obama's father and mother were both Communists, he officially and she by enthusiastic support for the Communist movement.

Obama has admitted that Frank Marshall Davis who was a friend of his grandfather is the mentor Frank in his book "Dreams of My Father"

Davis joined the Communist Party in the early 1940s; his Communist Party card number was 47544.

In a letter he sent to a friend during this time period, Davis wrote: "I've never discussed this with you and don't know whether you share the typical American uninformed concepts of Marxism or not, but I am risking such a reaction by saying that I have recently joined the Communist party."

The FBI first began tracking Davis in 1944, after having identified him as member of the Communist Party's Dorie Miller Club in Chicago. Over a nineteen-year span (1944-63), the Bureau compiled a 601-page file on Davis. One document therein suggests that Davis's CPUSA affiliations had begun as early as 1931. Moreover, the FBI listed Davis in its security index, meaning that he could be arrested or detained in the event of a national emergency.

In early 1945, the FBI identified Davis as a member of the Carver Second Ward West of the Communist Political Association. The following year, the Bureau identified him as a member of the Carver Club of the Communist Party. Davis' wife, meanwhile, was a member of the Paul Robeson Club of the Communist Party of Chicago.

Here's what another former Marxist who worked with Obama while at Occidental College in Los Angeles, on a Marxist revolution since 1980 has to say about Obama's commitment to Marxist revolution

> The election of Reagan was simply a minor set-back in terms of the coming revolution. As I recall, Obama repeatedly used the phrase "When the revolution comes...." In my mind, I remember thinking that Obama was blindly sticking to the simple Marxist theory that had characterized my own views while I was an undergraduate at Occidental College.

"There's going to be a revolution," Obama said, "we need to be organized and grow the movement." In Obama's view, our role must be to educate others so that we might usher in more quickly this inevitable revolution.

I know this may be implausible to some readers, but I distinctly remember Obama surprising me by bringing up Frantz Fanon and colonialism. He impressed me with his knowledge of these two topics, topics which were not among my strong points -- or of overwhelming concern to me. Boss and Obama seemed to think their ideological purity was a persuasive argument in predicting that a coming revolution would end capitalism. While I felt I was doing them a favor by providing them with the latest research, I saw I was in danger of being cast as a reactionary who did not grasp the nuances of international Marxist theory.

Chandoo let Boss and Obama take the crux of the argument to me. Chandoo, in fact, seemed chagrined by the level of disagreement in the group. I cannot remember him making any significant comments during this discussion. Drawing on the history of Western Europe, I responded it was unrealistic to think the working class would ever overthrow the capitalist system. As I recall, Obama reacted negatively to my critique, saying: "That's crazy!"

Since Boss and Obama had injected theory into our debate, I reacted by going historical. As best I can recreate the argument, I responded by critiquing their perspective with the fresh insight I had gained from my recent reading of Barrington Moore's book, Social Origins of Dictatorship and Democracy (1966). Moore had argued that a Russian or Chinese style revolution -- leading to communism -- was only possible in an agrarian society with a weak or non-existent middle-class or bourgeoisie.

Since I was a Marxist myself at the time, and had studied variations in Marxist theory, I can state that everything I heard Obama argue that evening was consistent with Marxist philosophy, including the ideas that class struggle was leading to an inevitable revolution and that an elite group of revolutionaries was needed to lead the effort. If he had not been a true Marxist-Leninist, I would have noticed and remembered. I can still, with some degree of ideological precision, identify which students at Occidental College were radicals and which ones were not. I can do the same thing for the Occidental College professors at that time.

By the time the debate came to an end, Obama -- although not Boss -- was making peace, agreeing with the facts I had laid out, and demonstrating an apparent agreement with my more realistic perspective. I have a vivid memory of Obama surrendering to my argument including signaling to the somewhat bewildered Chandoo -- through his voice and body language -- that the argument had concluded and had been decided in my favor. Around 9 p.m., Chandoo and Obama left for another appointment, either in Palo Alto or San Francisco. In retrospect, Obama had proved to me that he was indeed, as Boss had promised, "on our side."

Long before I realized Obama had grown into a spectacular political career, I have treasured this particular memory as an early example of my own intellectual growth and an early sign of my modest promise as a teacher. At the time, I had the impression that I might have been one of the first to directly challenge Obama's Marxist-Leninist mind-set and to introduce him to a more practical view that saw politics, rather than revolution, as the preferred route to socialism. Had I really persuaded him, or was he just making nice to smooth things over with a new friend? I'd like to think it was the former.

Whatever progress I made with Obama that evening, the price of our debate was a greater ideological wedge between me and Boss and a further decline in our rocky relationship. Our relationship would officially end in February and then flicker out completely by June 1981 -- much to the satisfaction of Boss's father.

I remember that Obama was friendly to me on at least three other occasions over the next several months. For example, Boss and I visited the apartment he shared with Chandoo. I spoke with him again on campus in the student union. I saw him on campus in The Cooler -- the school's coffee and sandwich shop. I also spoke with him at large party in June 1981. I certainly considered him a friend, a confidant and a political ally in the larger struggle against poverty and oppressive social systems.

Whatever impact our encounter might have had on him, I know something about what Barack Obama believed in 1980. At that time, the future president was a doctrinaire Marxist revolutionary, although perhaps -- for the first time -- considering conventional politics as a more practical road to socialism. Knowing this, I think I have a responsibility to place on the public record my account of this incident from our president's past.

John C. Drew, Ph.D. is an award-winning political scientist and a blogger at David Horowitz-s NewsReal Blog. Dr. Drew earned his Ph.D. from

Cornell and has taught political science and economics at Williams College.

http://www.Americanthinker.com/2011/02/ metting_young_obama.html

When Barack Obama moved to Illinois, he became active in Marxist Community Organizing. What many do not know, despite efforts of many of us for years, is that Obama ran for office in Illinois as a Socialist.

Obama was a member of the socialist New Party in Illinois. That is a published fact and beyond dispute. Here is the New Party link noting Obama as a New Party candidate for the Illinois State Senate seat that he won

http://chicagodsa.org/ngarchive/ng42.html/ #anchor792932

The New Party was formed and backed financially by the Democratic Socialists of America, thus making Obama also a member of the DSA

Here is what their founder Michael Harrington said

"Put it this way. Marx was a democrat with a small d. The Democratic Socialists envision a humane social order based on popular control of resources and production, economic planning...and racial equality. I share an immediate program with liberals in this country because the best liberalism leads toward socialism.... I want to be on the left wing of the possible."

Frank Marshall Davis continued directing Obama's connections to Communist and other leftist radicals including his friendship and support by Radical leftist terrorists Bill Ayers and Bernadette Dorn (Weather Underground)

Frank Marshall Davis also brought together Obama, Valerie Jarrett and David Axelrod

> Davis worked with the Canter family, who mentored David Axelrod. Davis also worked with Vernon Jarrett and Robert Taylor, father-in-law and grandfather to Valerie Jarrett. They all served together in Chicago's Communist Party circles in the 1940s.

http://www.breitbart.com/Big-Government/2012/08/08/Trioka-Obama-Axelrod-Jarrett

The Speakers at National Party Conventions are never chosen haphazardly. They are selected to either portray an image, project unity, or groom a pre-selected successor for the Presidency.

In 2004, that person was Barack Obama. His speech at the convention was praised by Democrats and the media. It powered him to victory that year in his Senate campaign over Conservative Black Republican Alan Keyes.

After a brief Senate career of no consequence,

Obama began his campaign for presidency in 2007. It is the conclusion of many political junkies including myself that Obama was groomed by the far left for this political run. They had in place all of the machinery to deny all the reports of his real past and to smear and/or destroy anyone who dared to speak the truth about him.

Even Joe Biden uttering one of his usual racist slurs only served to propel Obama forward.

> "I mean, you got the first mainstream African-American who is articulate and bright and clean and a nice-looking guy," Biden said. "I mean, that's a storybook, man."
> Biden issued a statement Wednesday afternoon, saying: "I deeply regret any offense my remark in the New York Observer might have caused anyone. That was not my intent and I expressed that to Sen. Obama."
> Biden also spoke to reporters in a conference call Wednesday afternoon and said the remark was taken out of context.
> "Barack Obama is probably the most exciting candidate that the Democratic or Republican Party has produced at least since I've been around," Biden said on the call. "And he's fresh. He's new. He's smart. He's insightful. And I really regret that some have taken totally out of context my use of the world 'clean.'"

<u>(Watch Biden's comments and Obama's reaction</u> 🔲)

Obama and the Democrats have commented for years now that one of Obama's signature legacy achievements was the Affordable Care Act (aka Obamacare).

This was transformational in that for the first time it required Americans to purchase a commercial product whether they wanted or needed it. This was the ultimate achievement of the destructive Wickard v Filburn Supreme Court Opinion mentioned earlier during the FDR Administration. To the shock of many Conservatives, Chief Justice Roberts issued the Majority Opinion in NFIB v. Sebelius (2012

NFIB v. Sebelius (2012)

Allowed Congress to force people to buy health insurance from private companies on the basis of the regulation being a "tax," by implication allowing Congress do virtually anything with the taxing power that no independent power, even the expansive Commerce Clause, would allow.

Chief Justice John Roberts cast the deciding vote affirming this decision in what was seen as an abandonment of judicial principles for the sake of maintaining an image of a moderating Court that is independent of political swings. He subsequently has even reversed himself on previous opinions that can only be attributed to the same view of the Court rather than interpreting the Constitution.

Obama and Immigration

To further expand upon his "Fundamental Transformation of America", Obama announced that he didn't need Congress to provide legislative changes he wanted. He announced via the press on January 20, 2014

> "I've got a pen and I've got a phone -- and I can use that pen to sign executive orders and take executive actions and administrative actions that move the ball forward," Obama said.

Obama had already demonstrated this by the Executive Order known as DACA (June 2012), allowing the children of illegal immigrants to not only stay in the United States, but to have legal authorization to work and to attend colleges.

He did this despite Congress rejecting in formal vote his request for legislation to make this immigration change.

Obama was signifying by actions what he had long stated. He made it clear he was a Wilsonian who rejected the language of the Constitution that it is the "Supreme Law of the Land" (Article VI, Clause 2).

Wilson put forth the ideology adopted by all Democrats since that the Constitution, rather than being the Ultimate or Supreme Law, is merely a "guideline", a course of suggestions. That is until a political opponent does something that they disagree with. Then it's "clear violation of Constitutional Law"

This transformational agenda by Obama was to set the stage for all the actions we have seen by the Democrats since he left office.

CHAPTER 8- THE NEW DEMOCRATIC PARTY- OLD SCHOOL FDR MARXIST FASCISTS AND NEW COMMUNISTS

The current Democratic Party and their media enablers like to use words like liberal or progressive to describe their current political ideology. But liberal is the wrong word for today's left. Their core beliefs are undeniably Marxist statist. Like Hitler, the Biden/Harris wing believes that pure communism is not the solution because it eliminates the state. Instead today's the Biden left shares with Fascism, Stalinism, and Nazism that the best implementation of Marxism is an all-powerful State that allows private enterprise under strict control of the state. This is so contrary to the values that made the United States the most powerful, most wealthy, and prosperous nation in the history of mankind. It's contrary to everything that drives immigrants from around the world to come here. They seek the opportunities that they know only the United States offers. That's why Democrats must never again be allowed the reins of power.

The Democrats, in this quest to complete Obama's "Fundamental Transformation" of the United States, employ two central tenets- Marxism's Essential steps to transition from Capitalism to Communism and Lenin's Democratic Collective Centralism

They are split in the "How". The Communist wing seeks the destruction of capitalism. The Fascist wing seeks to further FDR's embrace of fascism to control and manipulate capitalism and expand a welfare state.

The key belief within DCC or Democratic Collective Centralism is the belief of Collectivism.

"Collectivism being the idea of prioritizing the group rather than yourself or biased individuals such as your family. These prioritizations could be goals, outcomes, rights and so on.

This belief has been criticized for being 'inhuman' or 'unnatural' as people will naturally build biases towards individuals and parties. Socialists have argued the only way for this to work is to have common ownership.

The main or commonly spoken role which Collectivism plays within DCC is to shrink the wealth inequality within the public by having the significant majority of the population within the middle-class. This is done by the government enforcing strict tax laws within the state which effects low incomes very minorly however, large incomers significantly. The logic or reasoning behind the act is the belief that the money will have a better use if it's being used on the country's needs rather than materialistic needs. This relates to Collectivism as the money is being used for the public or the whole rather than individual "unnecessary materialistic needs."

In addition to taxation as key means of achieving these goals within Democratic Collective Centralism, there is the belief that when electing an individual you must vote for who you believe is the best for the state rather than who's best for you. This belief is practically impossible to enforce however, is seen as a moral.

DCC or Democratic Collective Centralism supports "free market of all private organizations" with one simple guideline. As long as the private organization is not intentionally damaging the country's or state's health for profit reasons, they're freely allowed to carry out all forms of legal business upon the public. However, if the private organization is found to be unintentionally damaging the country's or state's health when there is an option not to damage the country's or state's health; the government will step in and force that switch. All of this falls under collectivism because when the government acts, their reasoning will be for the ultimate benefit of the country or state.

Lastly, collectivism wants its people to prioritize the country's problems. What is meant by 'country's problems' could be the environment, science, unemployment and so on. The 'country's problems' can change dependent on the current situation. However, the key aspect to this belief is how citizens should view these problems. The people or citizens should embrace these beliefs and the "good of the state" as essential for the country's health or survival. This again links to Collectivism because of the aspect in prioritizing the country's problems."

With thanks to Market Socialism: The Debate Among Socialists, by Schweickart, David; Lawler, James; Ticktin, Hillel; Ollman, Bertell. 1998

Secondly and of critical importance is the Democrats adherence in what Marx called essential steps to transition from capitalism to communism found in Section II, Proletarians and Communists of the Communist Manifesto

1. Heavy Estate Taxes
2. Heavy Progressive Income Tax
3. Promote Unionism to destroy capitalism
4. Redefine family and destroy the concept of the traditional family and its influence.
5. Transfer as much power as possible to the Central State.
6. Free Public Education

http://www.constitution.org/tyr/
com_mani.htm#Proletarian

Third, is the shared view of Democrats with Hegel's the state is "god" that fits perfectly with Democratic Collective Centralism

What do I mean by Statism?

Statism is the belief that the civil government (or man via civil government) is the ultimate authority in the earth and as such is the source of law, morality, and righteousness (that which is right and wrong). Statism has manifested itself in different ways throughout history. It can be expressed through democratic and non-democratic governments alike.

A statist government treats its political sovereignty as a platform for moral sovereignty. In other words, as ultimate sovereign, the state is therefore not subject to God, the Bible, natural law, or any other religion or ethical system. A statist government need not be accountable to its own citizens. Rights under Statism come from the generosity of the State, and not inalienable from some mythical God. https://www.conservapedia.com/Statism

This section provides an objective analysis of the policies proposed and or already implemented by the Democrats and demonstrates that there is NO significant difference between the Democrats and the ideology of Marxist Statism.

All of these ideological positions are in diametric opposition to the Constitutional, small government established by our Founders.

Furthermore, we shall examine this ideological split into two wings, communists and fascists. Bernie Sanders and AOC (Alexandra Alexa Cortes) lead the communist wing, while Elizabeth Warren and Kamala Harris and puppet Joe are leading the Fascist wing. Fascism or National Socialism differs from Communism in that it sees a strong National State which also allows crony capitalism (putting it under strict Federal control). It also promotes federal unionism.

Back in the early 2000s the Progressive Caucus of the Democratic Party proudly claimed their membership in the Democratic Socialists of America. That is until we Conservatives began publicizing that membership and they took it down from their Congressional Page.

The Progressive Caucus was founded in 1991 by then-freshman Congressman Bernie Sanders, a longtime affiliate of the country's largest Marxist organization, the Democratic Socialists of America (DSA). Caucus co-founders included DSA member Ron Dellums (D-Calif.), DSA-aligned Lane Evans (D-Ill.), and DSA/CPUSA-friendly Maxine Waters (D-Calif.).

In 1999, the youth wing of the DSA, the Young Democratic Socialists of James Madison University, wrote:

DSA. [sic] is not a political party, but rather works within the left wing of the Democratic Party and other third parties. DSA. [sic] is a driving force for the Progressive Caucus in the U.S. House of Representatives (led by Rep. Bernie Sanders, Socialist Congressman of Vermont).

The Democratic Socialists of the USA boast of their allegiance to and the close relationship of the Democratic Party to them. Nearly all the members of the Progressive Caucus are also members of the DSUSA. This was noted on the Progressive Caucus website up until 2004 when they took it down as people like myself began posting it.

Here is the list from 2004 before it was removed

The Democratic Socialists of America, Progressive Caucus members lists the following elected Representatives in the US House of Representatives as members (as of 2004):

OFFICERS Dennis Kucinich (CO-CHAIR, OHIO-10) Barbara Lee (CO-CHAIR, CALIFORNIA-09) Lynn Woolsey (VICE-CHAIR, CALIFORNIA-06) Peter DeFazio (OFFICER, OREGON-04) Jesse Jackson, Jr (OFFICER, ILLINOIS-02) Major Owens (OFFICER, NEW YORK-11) Bernie Sanders (OFFICER, VERMONT) Hilda Solis (OFFICER, CALIFORNIA-31)

MEMBERS Neil Abercrombie (HI-01), Tammy Baldwin (WI-02), Xavier Becerra (CA-30), David Bonior (MI-10), Corrine Brown (FL-03), Sherrod

Brown (OH-13), Michael Capuano (MA-08), Julia Carson (IN-10), William Clay (MO-01), John Conyers (MI-14), Danny Davis (IL-07), Peter DeFazio (OR-04), Rosa DeLauro (CT-03), Lane Evans (IL-17), Eni Faleomavaega (American Samoa), Sam Farr (CA-17), Chaka Fattah (PA-02), Bob Filner (CA-50), Barney Frank (MA-04), Luis Gutierrez (IL-04), Earl Hilliard (AL-07), Maurice Hinchey (NY-26), Jesse Jackson, Jr. (IL-02), Sheila Jackson-Lee (TX-18), Stephanie Tubbs Jones (OH-11), Marcy Kaptur (OH-09), Tom Lantos (CA-12), John Lewis (GA-05), Jim McDermott (WA-07), James P. McGovern (MA-03), Carrie Meek (FL-17), George Miller (CA-07), Patsy Mink (HI-02), Jerry Nadler (NY-08), Eleanor Holmes Norton (DC), John Oliver (MA-01), Ed Pastor (AZ-02), Donald Payne (NJ-10)., Nancy Pelosi (CA-08), Jan Schakowski (IL-09), Jose Serrany (NY-16), Hilds Solis (CA-31), Pete Stark (CA-13), Bennie Thompson (MS-02), John Tierney (MA-06), Tom Udall (NM-03), Nydia Velazquez (NY-12), Maxine Waters (CA-35), Mel Watt (NC-12), Henry Waxman (CA-29), Lynn Woolsey (CA-06)

Do not make the mistake of under-estimating the Socialist Revolutionary Commitment of AOC and others.

These Socialists today are divided into two camps. Those who believe that through organizing and political strikes they can destroy capitalism, and those who see that as only the opening effort that must be concluded with violent revolution.

"Bhaskar Sunkara, the young, left, entrepreneurial genius who founded and publishes Jacobin, has written a book, The Socialist Manifesto, in which he puts himself forward as the spokesperson for his generation's socialist movement in America. He is certainly in a credible position to do so. His magazine Jacobin has the largest circulation both in print and online of any left publication in many decades, and for those who want something deeper he also publishes Catalyst: A Journal of Theory and Strategy. And if you don't have time to read, there is also Jacobin radio. He is an important figure, though not an elected officer, in the Democratic Socialists of America or DSA, a group that now has more than 60,000 members, the largest left organization since the Communist Party of the 1940s. Bhaskar's publications can claim credit for attracting and educating many of them. He is a public figure. He is profiled in and writes opinion pieces for The New York Times and interviewed in its podcasts. And his pieces appear in The Guardian as well. During the last several years, Bhaskar had become American socialism's public face.

The political heart of the Socialist Manifesto is to

be found in Part II, the last fifty pages, where the author lays out his political strategy for today. Bhaskar contrasts social democracy to what he sees as the alternative: democratic socialism. By democratic socialism, he means a more militant, class-struggle movement that through labor union organization, winning increasing political power in state legislatures and Congress, as well as through social protests, and political strikes will bring about a transformational change. Bhaskar recognizes that social democracy failed, but he believes that today the struggles of the left must take place principally within the old social democratic parties. Or in some cases the democratic socialists can work in new broad left parties such as Podemos in Spain. As he writes in an interesting and problematic formulation, "Class struggle social democracy, then, isn't a foe of democratic socialism—the road to the latter runs through the former."

https://newpol.org/the-socialist-manifesto-of-bhaskar-sunkara-of-jacobin-socialism-without-revolution/

https://jacobinmag.com/2019/07/revolutionary-socialism-party-strategy

https://jacobinmag.com/2019/07/socialism-progressives-liberalism

https://socialistrevolution.org

Democrats use to hide and deny their Marxist

ideology and membership in both the DSUSA and the CPUSA. Since 2018 this is now an open relationship with the Progressive Caucus in Congress and at State and Local Government levels.

Note this 2019 report on the assimilation of the Communist Party into the Democratic Party. The link at the end provides a lot more detail on involvement by many members of Congress and staffers including staffers for Joe Biden. This report was produced by Trevor Loudon for the New American.

> "The current Congress could become the most radical in American history. Once-marginalized "progressives," socialists, and even Communist Party supporters are taking the reins of several strategic congressional committees. Democratic Party leadership is bending to accommodate fired-up young radicals.
>
> Socialists have been infiltrating the Democratic Party for decades — and the Republican Party on occasion. The situation has gotten gradually worse since the Vietnam War era. Democratic Party "moderates" have been mostly successful — with the help of the establishment media — in keeping a lid on their socialist wing for years, but the relentless pressure from open socialists, along with an increasingly indoctrinated populace, has finally blown the lid off the charade. Every election cycle the radicals have gained a little more ground. In 2018, a

tipping point was reached. Mere "infiltration" is boiling over into a full-fledged scarlet-tinged socialist takeover.

Of course, there is no open "Communist Party Caucus" in the U.S. Congress, but the ties to the Communist Party USA (CPUSA) are undeniable. Our survey of the socialist revolution in Congress begins by referencing communist acknowledgements of their congressional influence, followed by a hard look at each of the major Democrat caucuses, with further documentation showing communist connections to the Congressional Progressive Caucus in particular. Then we list the various expected committee heads (this survey is going to the printer on January 3, the first day of the new Congress), encapsulating their radical connections. To make our case ironclad, our survey is necessarily detailed. This is intended not as "pleasure reading" but as an irrefutable wake-up call, and should be shared.

Quad Caucus members willingly work with the 5,000 members of Communist Party USA to broaden government programs, change U.S. foreign policy, and cut military spending.

According to an April 2010 CPUSA Political Action Commission Report submitted as part of the discussion leading up to the party's 29th National Convention May 21-23, 2010:

The formation this year of the Quad

Caucus within Congress is a reflection of a growing demographic and progressive shift within the electorate. The collaboration of the Congressional Black, Hispanic, Asian-Pacific and Progressive caucuses creates a strong counter-force to the conservative element within the Democratic Party.

Many of our clubs are located in Congressional Districts of Quad Caucus members. A labor-people's electoral force working within the broad alliance and relating with members of Congress can project specific legislation like passage of the Local Jobs for America Act to restore one million jobs in cities and towns, and bigger goals like shifting military funding to human needs with massive public works job creation.

A report highlighting the CPUSA's connection to the Congressional Progressive Caucus, often referred to as the "Progressive Caucus," was delivered at the 14th International Meeting of Communist and Workers' Parties, held in Beirut, Lebanon, from November 22 to 25, 2012, by the late Erwin Marquit, a then-member of the CPUSA's International Department:

The Communist Party USA not only welcomes the reelection of President Barack Obama, but actively engaged in the electoral campaign for his reelection and for the election of many Democratic Party congressional candidates....

In our electoral policy, we seek to cooperate

and strengthen our relationship with the more progressive elements in [the] Democratic Party, such as the Progressive Caucus....

The Progressive Caucus was founded in 1991 by then-freshman Congressman Bernie Sanders, a longtime affiliate of the country's largest Marxist organization, the Democratic Socialists of America (DSA). Caucus co-founders included DSA member Ron Dellums (D-Calif.), DSA-aligned Lane Evans (D-Ill.), and DSA/CPUSA-friendly Maxine Waters (D-Calif.).

In 1999, the youth wing of the DSA, the Young Democratic Socialists of James Madison University, wrote:

DSA. [sic] is not a political party, but rather works within the left wing of the Democratic Party and other third parties. DSA. [sic] is a driving force for the Progressive Caucus in the U.S. House of Representatives (led by Rep. Bernie Sanders, Socialist Congressman of Vermont).

The Democratic Socialists' relationship with the Congressional Progressive Caucus remains strong to this day. At 55,000 members, DSA has the electoral muscle to make even entrenched "moderate" Democrats tremble.

California Congressman and DSA-friendly Ro Khanna is now first vice-chair of the CPC, while Alexandria Ocasio-Cortez is both a very vocal new member of the Progressive Caucus and a card-carrying DSA member.

Back in February 2002, Joelle Fishman, chair

of the Political Action Committee-CPUSA, evaluated the usefulness of the Congressional Progressive Caucus in a report to the party's National Board:

Although this Caucus [CPC] is not large enough to control the Congressional agenda ... the existence of this group of 57 members of Congress ... provides an important lever that can be used to advance workers' issues and move the debate to the left in every Congressional District in the country.

Buoyed by an influx of new far-left members, the CPC has made a bargain with Democratic House leader Nancy Pelosi (herself a former CPC member) to significantly increase socialist power in the House of Representatives. The deal will see more CPUSA and DSA-aligned members of Congress appointed to key congressional committees, empowering them to gain even greater influence over legislative priorities."

https://www.thefreelibrary.com/The+Looming +Socialist+Revolution+on+Capitol+Hill%3a +For+the+first+time%2c...-a0572716091

THE BERNIE SANDERS TRANSFORMATION OF THE DEMOCRATIC PARTY TO A FULL BLOWN MARXIST PARTY

From a January 2020 Huffington Post Article

Joe Biden said in the recent debate with President Trump that he is the head of the Democratic Party. However, any rational analysis shows that Bernie Sanders is the ideological head of the Democratic Party

Vermont senator and Democratic presidential candidate Bernie Sanders once said that he was "physically nauseated" by a speech made by President John F. Kennedy when Sanders was a young man, because Kennedy's "hatred for the Cuban Revolution [...] was so strong."

Sen. Bernie Sanders (I-Vt.) once told a fellow left-wing activist that the Democratic Party was too "intellectually bankrupt" to allow the progressive movement to flourish within it.

In a 1985 letter newly obtained by HuffPost in which Sanders debated running for governor, he wrote: "Whether I run for governor or not is really not important. What would be a tragedy, however, is for people with a radical vision to fall into the pathetic camp of the intellectually bankrupt Democratic Party."

Times have changed.

Sanders, who has served as an independent in Congress — first in the House and now in the Senate — since 1991, is now among the leading Democratic candidates for president, second behind former Vice President Joe Biden in national polls, and tied for first in Iowa. He's raised more money than any other candidate in the Democratic primary, with more individual contributions. His platform — which includes "Medicare for All," tuition-free college, and wealth redistribution through aggressive taxes on the richest Americans — defines the party's progressive wing.

Source: Huffington Post January 18, 2020

Let's begin with the signature issue of Sanders' campaign: a national single-payer health-care program, or Medicare-for-all as it's known.

Hillary Clinton, who ultimately bested Sanders for the party's nomination, insisted the idea "will never, ever come to pass." Fast forward roughly a year, and Sanders' proposed Medicare-for-all legislation attracted 16 Democratic co-spoinsors, including likely presidential contenders Sens. Elizabeth Warren (D-Mass.), Corey Booker (D-N.J.), Kirsten Gillibrand (D-N.Y.), and eventual Vice Presidential nominee, Kamala Harris (D-Calif.).

THE MYTH OF THE
MODERATE JOE BIDEN

Joe Biden has for decades cultivated an image as a supposedly "moderate" Democrat. During his Senate years, he certainly had "accomplishments that would lead one to draw that conclusion. His attacks on Social Security, his loyalty to the Banks, Credit Card Companies, and the Pharmaceutical Industry are well established. But He was also more than willing to accommodate leftist ideology, especially regarding abortion, taxation, and redistribution of wealth programs. But his leftist credentials became firmly established as Vice President under Barack Obama.

It was Joe Biden who pushed Obama to embrace Homosexual Marriage after both had long been on record as opposing this move. It was Biden who became unwilling to embrace an aggressive stance against Islamic Jihad, against the atrocities in Syria, and Iranian aggression.

When Biden began his quest for the Democratic Presidential nomination in the 2020 campaign, he still tried to play the moderate card. But as it became evident that the power rested with the radical Sanders leftists, Biden made the calculation that he could not win unless he fully embraced the left.

Biden promised Sanders that he would have the most progressive (leftist) Administration since FDR.

"Joe Biden: (34:12)
As I've said for a long time, when we do that, we'll not only do the hard work of rebuilding this nation, we can transform this nation. We can transform it so that it goes down in history with your help, Bernie, as one of the most progressive administrations since Roosevelt. And I really believe, I think it's doable because the whole world has changed. It's not just us. The whole world has changed. We're in the middle of a fourth industrial revolution. The question is, will there be a middle class left based on all that's happening? We have to address it. It's not just our concern. If we, the wealthiest country in the world, can't address it and provide more equity and opportunity, we're going to continue to see the kind of shifts you see in Europe."
https://www.rev.com/blog/transcripts/transcript-bernie-sanders-endorses-joe-biden-in-livestream-meeting

However, when you examine the policy platform of Biden, what we see is that Biden and the so-called "moderate Democrats" embrace a mix of the Sanders Communist ideology and FDR Marxist Fascism. The following section discusses Biden's official record or promises regarding many of the issues dividing our country.

Fossil Fuels

Former Vice President Joe Biden claimed during a campaign event that "we're all dead" if fossil fuels continue to be used as one of the world's primary energy sources.

Biden made the apocalyptic pronouncement while discussing climate change before a crowd of supporters in Peterborough, New Hampshire

> "If we don't stop using fossil fuels–" an attendee began a question to the candidate.

> "We're all dead," Biden interrupted.

Earlier in the event, Biden vowed as president to hold energy giants liable for global warming and made a pledge to even jail executives.

> "We have to set sort of guide rails down now, so between the years 2021 and 2030, it's irreversible – the path we set ourselves on. And one of which is doing away with any substance for fossil fuels – number one," Biden said.

> "In order to curb the rate of pollution, Biden explained, we need to hold fossil fuel executives "liable for what they have done, particularly in those cases where there are underserved neighborhoods."

> When they don't deliver, Biden offered, "put them in jail."

> December 29, 2019 Peterborough New

MR LARRY ROBINSON

Hampshire

BIDEN CALLS FOR BANNING FIREARMS

Biden recently called for banning the two most owned firearms used for self-defense (especially by women)

"While saying he supports the Second Amendment, Biden called the absolutist arguments of some gun-rights supporters "bizarre." Noting people can't own machine guns or bazookas, Biden said:

"Why should we allow people to have military-style weapons including pistols with 9-mm bullets and can hold 10 or more rounds?"

https://www.lawenforcementtoday.com/joe-biden-ban-9mm-pistols-just-like-we-ban-bazookas-and-machine-guns/

https://www.dailywire.com/news/joe-biden-essentially-calls-for-banning-nearly-all-firearms

Biden goes further to specifically promise to disarm church goers

https://winteryknight.com/2019/09/03/joe-biden-promises-to-confiscate-all-multi-round-magazines-disarm-church-goers/

BIDEN PROMISES TO CUT
BACK THE MILITARY

In the current presidential campaign, Joe Biden would have you believe he has always and will always support for our military. Further he falsely claims that he will maintain our military
This is what he said in January 2020.

> On the relationship between the United States and China, Biden said he did not count China as a competitor. Instead, the United States "should be helping, and benefiting ourselves by doing that."
>
> "But the idea that China is going to eat our lunch, it was like I remembered debates in the late '90s, remember Japan was going to own us? Give me a break," he said."
>
> https://youtu.be/l_t7R_ImyQg
>
> "So, the idea we're gonna cut the defense budget significantly, we can cut it some, but we don't need standing armies, we need to be smarter than we're dealing now into how we handle this," he continued.
>
> https://youtu.be/Vf-5SeWwPxs

Biden says we do not need a standing army and that instead we should spend on helping Communist China.

https://thebl.com/us-news/joe-biden-we-dont-need-standing-armies-we-should-be-helping-communist-china.html

BIDEN- FREE HEALTHCARE
FOR ILLEGALS

NBC moderator Savannah Guthrie pressed former Vice President Joe Biden on the subject after failing to see that he raised his hand with the other candidates. When asked by Guthrie if he would provide federally supported health coverage to undocumented immigrants, Biden quickly corrected her.

> You cannot let people who are sick, no matter where they come from, no matter what their status, go uncovered. You can't do that. It's just going to be taken care of. Period. You have to. It's the humane thing to do," he insisted. (Bolton, 6/27)

BIDEN NOW SUPPORTS TAXPAYER FUNDED ABORTIONS

"Biden has still faced plenty of criticism from the left for his policies. Shortly after beginning his campaign, <u>he was forced to reverse </u>his previous support for the so-called Hyde Amendment, which banned federal funding for abortions."

https://www.mcclatchydc.com/news/politics-government/election/campaigns/article234890482.html#storylink=cpy

Biden and the Democratic Party have also embraced Sander's insistence on the following issues and they are incorporated into the Democratic Party Platform and/or the Biden/Sanders Manifesto

$15.00 An Hour Federal Minimum Wage

Free College For All-

"Make public colleges and universities tuition-free for all families with incomes below $125,000. Biden has long said that when it comes to public education in America, we're starting too late and ending too soon — and that if we were building the public education system in America today it would extend from pre-k, starting with 3 and 4

year olds through ensuring 16 years of education is affordable. Biden has added to his education beyond high school agenda by adopting Senator Sanders' proposal to make public colleges and universities tuition-free for all students whose family incomes are below $125,000.

https://www.latimes.com/politics/ story/2020-03-15/biden-adopts-part-progressive-agenda-seeks-unify-party

Healthcare Is A Right

Housing is a right

Guaranteed Paid Sick leave for everyone including the self-employed.

"That is why Democrats commit to forging a new social and economic contract with the American people—a contract that invests in the people and promotes shared prosperity, not one that benefits only big corporations and the wealthiest few.

A new contract that recognizes all Americans have a right to quality, affordable health care. One that affirms housing is a right and not a privilege"

Paid sick leave is a necessity even under normal circumstances, but in a pandemic, it's a matter of national security. We will immediately enact robust paid sick leave protections as part of the COVID-19 response for all workers in the economy, including contractors, gig workers, domestic workers, and the self-employed.

Democratic Party Platform 2020

Open Borders Party

The far Left Mother Jones Magazine acknowledges Democrats want Open Borders

"Are Democrats Now the Party of Open Borders?
I have previously criticized Republicans who accused liberals of wanting "open borders." President Trump tweets about this endlessly. But I have to admit that it's hard to see much daylight between Warren's plan and de facto open borders. As near as I can tell, CBP will be re-tasked away from patrolling the border looking for illegal crossings; if border officers happen to apprehend someone, they'll be released almost immediately; if they bother to show up for their court date, they'll have a lawyer appointed for them; and employers will have no particular reason to fear giving them a job.
Am I missing something here? Does Warren's plan explicitly make it vanishingly unlikely that anyone crossing our border will ever be caught and sent back?
The whole thing is very similar to Julian Castro's plan.
https://www.motherjones.com/kevin-drum/2019/07/are-democrats-now-the-party-of-open-borders/

No reasonable person would conclude that these are "moderate", centrist positions. All are far to the left of even the Obama Administration.

CHAPTER 9-
CONCLUSIONS

So after journeying with me through a brief but detailed chronology of the Democratic Party, how do we come to understand it and its goals?

You have to begin by understanding the driving force behind Collectivism. It goes back throughout the history of mankind to visions of creating a Utopian Society.

Mark Levin wrote an excellent book on this entitled, Ameritopia, The Unmaking of America. He goes through the history of those seeking to create a Utopian Society. It ALWAYS has required the tyranny of the majority to enforce its will upon the minority.

Excerpted from Chapter 1 of Ameritopia

> Tyranny, broadly defined, is the use of power to dehumanize the individual and delegitimize his nature. Political utopianism is tyranny disguised as a desirable, workable, and even paradisiacal governing ideology."

Plato's *Republic*, More's *Utopia*, Hobbes's *Leviathan*, and Marx's workers' paradise are utopias that are anti-individual and anti-individualism. For the utopians, modern and olden, the individual is one-dimensional—selfish. On his own, he has little moral value. Contrarily, authoritarianism is defended as altruistic and masterminds as socially conscious. Thus endless interventions in the individual's life and manipulation of his conditions are justified as not only necessary and desirable but noble governmental pursuits. This false dialectic is at the heart of the problem we face today.

In truth, man is naturally independent and self-reliant, which are attributes that contribute to his own well-being and survival, and the well-being and survival of a civil society. He is also a social being who is charitable and compassionate. History abounds with examples, as do the daily lives of individuals. To condemn individualism as the utopians do is to condemn the very foundation of the civil society and the American founding and endorse, wittingly or unwittingly, oppression. Karl Popper saw it as an attack on Western civilization. "The emancipation of the individual was indeed the great spiritual revolution which had led to the breakdown of tribalism and to the rise of democracy." Moreover, Judaism and Christianity, among other religions, teach the altruism of the individual.

As Plato argued in his "Republic," utopians believe the individual must subordinate his will to the state. They must destroy individuality and individual liberty because those stand in opposition to the conformity their utopian vision demands.

Standing in stark contrast are America's constitutional framers, who rejected the folly that certain superior representatives of the species could change the entire species' intrinsic nature. They believed in man's natural rights and cherished the individual liberty flowing from those rights.

As students of history, philosophy and human nature, they refused to follow the path of utopians who rejected the realities not only of human nature but also of the evidence of its outworkings in history, especially in man's endless experiments in statecraft.

With wide-eyed recognition of human nature, they crafted the American Constitution to maximize individual liberties, despite the natural tendency of man toward absolutism.

As the Constitution established that essential balance between governmental power and individual liberties by sufficiently empowering but also limiting governmental power, it is essential that its structure be maintained if our freedom is to be preserved.

Utopian leftists view the Constitution not as a structural safeguard for our liberties, but as an obstacle to their utopian goal of concentrating power in the central government to empower them to implement their grand vision. They only champion the Constitution as a matter of political expedience, when it serves their larger ends."

Ameritopia: The Unmaking of America, by Mark R. Levin. New York: Threshold Editions, 2012. 288 pp

This Utopian Statist Collectivism ideology is at its core, the ideology of tyranny. It matters not whether it is well intentioned or not. As CS Lewis noted

Of all tyrannies, a tyranny exercised for the good of its victims may be the most oppressive. It may be better to live under robber barons than under omnipotent moral busybodies. The robber baron's cruelty may sometimes sleep, his cupidity may at some point be satiated; but those who torment us for our own good will torment us without end, for they do so with the approval of their own conscience.

C.S. Lewis

One of the essential characteristics of Collectivism is a focus on group identity rather than the individual.

We see this played out daily with Racial, Ethnic, Gender, and Class identity as the focus of the Democrat Collectivists

They insist on breaking society into different tribes based on uncontrollable characteristics such as race, gender, skin color, sexuality and the list goes on and on. According to the left, you should mainly be focused on your group identity and the needs of the group, to sculpt your opinions and beliefs.

What are the solutions?

As I indicated throughout this book. This move towards Statist Collectivism and away from our Founding Principles of individualism and Limited Government has been in process for more than 100 years. This did not come upon us since Barack Obama.

Furthermore, the Establishment Republicans have had no issue with this change. They are happy with Big Government controlling our lives and businesses. Their difference with the Democrats is that they have deceived themselves and many voters into believing that they would simply be more efficient managers of Statist Collectivism. Further, that they would SLOW the move towards eventual Communism instead of rushing towards it as the Democrats have.

The simple and straightforward answer is that first, Americans must not merely defeat the Democrats, they must be totally crushed at the polling booth.

Not because I wish to see a multiparty system eliminated. But we need to have the major parties at least be reflective of our Constitution, its principles and the values that our Framers and Founders said were essential for the longevity of this

Constitutional Republic

Secondly, we must elect individuals who are committed to the principles of individualism and natural rights that our Founders premised this Constitutional Republic. That is enhanced by our sense of greater equality of opportunity, regardless of race, ethnic background, or gender.

Third as our Founders and most Politicians prior to the Post JFK era stated, our nation's values must be anchored in a moral foundation. Their words are not a claim or requirement that all citizens must be Christians. They are stating that our VALUES, our LAWS and JUSTICE are anchored by Biblical Principles

Joseph Story

U. S. Congressman; "Father of American Jurisprudence"; U. S. Supreme Court Justice Appointed By President James Madison

"One of the beautiful boasts of our municipal jurisprudence is that Christianity is a part of the Common Law. There never has been a period in which the Common Law did not recognize Christianity as lying at its foundations.

I verily believe that Christianity is necessary to support a civil society and shall ever attend to its institutions and acknowledge its precepts as the pure and natural sources of private and social happiness."

George Washington

"Of all the dispositions and habits which lead to political prosperity, religion and morality are indispensable supports. In vain would that man claim the tribute of patriotism who should labor to subvert these great pillars of human happiness, these firmest props of the duties of man and citizens. The mere politician, equally with the pious man, ought to respect and to cherish them. A volume could not trace all their connexions with private and public felicity. Let it simply be asked, Where is the security for property, for reputation, for life, if the sense of religious obligation desert the oaths, which are the instruments of investigation in Courts of Justice? And let us with caution indulge the supposition that morality can be maintained without religion. Whatever may be conceded to the influence of refined education on minds of peculiar structure, reason and experience both forbid us to expect that national morality can prevail in exclusion of religious principle. It is substantially true, that virtue or morality is a necessary spring of popular government. The rule, indeed, extends with more or less force to every species of free government. Who, that is a sincere friend to it, can look with indifference upon attempts to shake the foundation of the fabric?" -

George Washington's Farewell Address, September 19, 1796

Noah Webster

Revolutionary Soldier; Judge; Legislator; Educator; "Schoolmaster to America":

[T]he religion which has introduced civil liberty is the religion of Christ and His apostles... This is genuine Christianity and to this we owe our free constitutions of government.

The moral principles and precepts found in the Scriptures ought to form the basis of all our civil constitutions and laws.

[O]ur citizens should early understand that the genuine source of correct republican principles is the Bible, particularly the New Testament, or the Christian religion.

[T]he Christian religion is the most important and one of the first things in which all children under a free government ought to be instructed. No truth is more evident than that the Christian religion must be the basis of any government intended to secure the rights and privileges of a free people.

The Bible is the chief moral cause of all that

is good and the best corrector of all that is evil in human society – the best book for regulating the temporal concerns of men.

[T]he Christian religion... is the basis, or rather the source, of all genuine freedom in government... I am persuaded that no civil government of a republican form can exist and be durable in which the principles of Christianity have not a controlling influence.

Daniel Webster

U. S. Senator; Secretary of State; "Defender of the Constitution":

The Christian religion – its general principles – must ever be regarded among us as the foundation of civil society.

Whatever makes men good Christians, makes them good citizens.

[T]o the free and universal reading of the Bible... men [are] much indebted for right views of civil liberty.

> The Bible is a book... which teaches man his own individual responsibility, his own dignity, and his equality with his fellow man.

President Harry Truman

"The fundamental basis of this nation's laws was given to Moses on the Mount. The fundamental basis of our Bill of Rights comes from the teachings we get from Exodus and

Saint Matthew, from Isaiah and Saint Paul. I don't think we emphasize that enough these days. If we don't have a proper fundamental moral background, we will finally end up with a totalitarian government which does not believe in rights for anybody except the State!"-- President Harry Truman February 15, 1950 Speech at the Department of Justice Department

John F Kennedy

Our government was founded on the essential religious idea of integrity of the individual. It was this religious sense which inspired the authors of the Declaration of Independence:

The American character has been not only religious, idealistic, and patriotic, but because of these it has been essentially individual".

Today these basic religious ideas are challenged by atheism and materialism: at home in the cynical philosophy of many of our intellectuals, abroad in the doctrine of collectivism, which sets up the twin pillars of atheism and materialism as the official philosophical establishment of the State.

John F Kennedy Independence Day Speech, July 4th 1946

So thank you readers for investing in this examination. Now the rest is up to YOU. As free citizens we have the privilege and responsibility to choose what kind of government and society we desire to live under.

Let me conclude with these thoughts from the Framers on what constitutes a nation of liberty

This philosophy of natural rights was championed by such Founding Fathers as Samuel Adams, Richard Bland, Patrick Henry, Thomas Jefferson, Richard Henry Lee, James Madison, George Mason, Robert Carter, Nicholas, Peyton Randolph, George Washington, and George Wythe.

Indeed, it would be amazing if any Revolutionary leader of the Commonwealth could be found who did not subscribe to the doctrines of natural law and right. Moreover, the doctrine was not limited to the select few who directed Virginia's destinies, but was widely held and continually expressed by the popular assemblages throughout the Commonwealth during Revolutionary days.

In their most generalized expressions the Founding Fathers spoke of their natural rights to life and liberty, adding at times, property, and on other occasions, the pursuit of happiness. To some contemporaries the alternative use of property and the pursuit of happiness may seem strange, but to many of the Fathers property meant the right to develop one's properties, that is, his faculties. The particular natural rights on which there was the largest measure of agreement among the Virginians were

(1) freedom of conscience

(2) freedom of communication

(3) the right to be free from arbitrary laws

(4) the rights of assembly and petition

(5) the property right

(6) the right of self-government, to which were frequently appended (a) the right of expatriation and (b) a right to change the form of government.

Thomas Jefferson in his Notes on Virginia,

> Jefferson wrote: "And can the liberties of a nation be thought secure when we have removed their only firm basis, a conviction in the minds of the people that these liberties are the gift of God?" Speaking there of our natural rights, he concluded:

"We are answerable for them to our God."' It was in the Summary View in which Jefferson asserted that Parliament had no power to encroach "upon those rights which God and the laws have given equally and independently to all."

Knowledge is essential to good decision making. I have attempted to give the citizens of this country that I love and have served with the knowledge necessary to choose well.

Larry Robinson